Last Gasps

Edited by Paul Collins and Meredith Costain

Read all of the
 **Thrillogy** Titles

Published by Sundance Publishing
P.O. Box 1326, 234 Taylor Street, Littleton, MA 01460

Copyright in individual stories remains with the authors.

First published 1999 as Spinouts by
Addison Wesley Longman Australia Pty Limited
95 Coventry Street, South Melbourne 3205 Australia
Exclusive United States Distribution: Sundance Publishing

ISBN 0-7608-4833-5

Printed in Canada

Contents

Past Midnight

The author
Glyn Parry
talks about the story

"*Past Midnight* came to me after riding the ghost train at an amusement park. It was the biggest rip-off, not scary at all. Where were the ghosts? Later I caught the last train out of the city, and I had my answer."

Past Midnight

They boarded the train just after 8:30 p.m.

"It's Friday night," Larry had said earlier, at his place. "All street gangs go out on Friday nights."

So now they tried to look tough. Jarvo chewed gum. Spike bounced. Steve looked nervous. An ancient weirdo sat at the end of the car.

"Get moving!" Helen pushed them forward.

"Look at these dead people everywhere," said Jodee. "Can't the city afford to bury them?"

No one noticed the weirdo walk over.

"Ah, the night belongs to the young." He wore a knee-length coat and wide-brimmed hat. His voice sounded paper-thin.

"Hey, pal, why don't you just — "

Jarvo stopped short. Their visitor gave him such a fierce look.

"Gather in, friends." He sat and faced the gang. His face softened. "I have a task for you to perform."

"I am old, yes?" The stranger chose his words carefully. "In Europe my family survived for generations. They were wanderers. They knew tricks."

Jodee and Helen sat mesmerized. In fact, they all did.

"But the persecutions changed everything."

The train lumbered through the suburbs.

"I fled to your country and worked hard, yes? Soon I had my first amusement park ride. You young people, you like the rides, yes?"

"Park rides?" said Larry. "Oh, yeah, we love 'em."

A thin hand, paler than the moon, reached deep inside the coat pocket to produce a hundred dollar bill. More money followed.

The spell was broken.

"Five hundred bucks!" Jarvo scanned every face. "That's a lot of cash."

"Everything is relative," said the weirdo. "Call it an old man's pleasure, if you like."

"You said something about performing a task." Larry leaned closer.

The old man's dark eyes narrowed. All softness disappeared. "The old amusement park, the one they closed down?"

"I know it," said Spike. "Two stations past Central."

Steve's mind drifted. Wasn't that place supposed to be haunted?

"Some kids are missing," continued Spike. "The cops don't have a clue."

The stranger sighed. "Last year six children climbed over the wall, never to be seen again."

"Sounds scary," said Helen.

"Precisely." The old man put his money away. "That's why the park never reopened. And now the authorities want to squeeze the owner out. They want the land, you see."

"Hey, how come you know so much?" Larry interrupted. "You seem to know a lot."

"Because I *am* the owner."

Central Station blurred into view.

"You want to pay us five hundred bucks to go there tonight?"

"It will be yours to keep," said the stranger. "If you stay until midnight."

Steve smelled a rat. "Okay, but why?"

"Oh, I just want to see the rides work one last time. But there's one condition."

"What condition?" quizzed Jarvo.

"Simply this: you must not ride the ghost train after midnight."

"That's dumb."

"Granted, but that's the condition."

Steve spoke up. "What about before midnight?"

"Before doesn't matter. Please yourselves. But after . . ."

He stood up to go. They watched him move down the aisle.

"Hey, what about the money?" Larry yelled after the old man

"You'll be paid."

"Will you be there?"

"But of course, young man. You can bet your life on it."

The train stopped and the weirdo got off. Central Station was busy. With his collar raised and his hat drawn down, the stranger dissolved into the Friday night crowd.

Two stations later, they were on their way. It took ten minutes to reach the old amusement park. They followed a red brick path all the way to iron gates.

Spike shoved hard, then jumped back in surprise.

"They're not locked!"

Somewhere unseen, electric generators hummed. A colored bulb winked. More lights came on. Deep behind the wall, the park flickered into life.

"Hey, wait a sec." Steve hung back. "You're not going in there?"

Larry turned on him. "We came all this way, dummy."

Spike pointed to the rides beyond. "All ours!"

"Plus five hundred big ones," said Jarvo.

Steve didn't budge. "Yeah, but look what happened to the last bunch."

"That was different." Larry thumbed the brickwork. "They broke in. We were invited."

It was enough. Helen and Jodee squeezed through the turnstile. Everyone followed.

"There's the ghost train." Larry pointed.

"Later," said Jarvo. "Hey, Spike, you see what I see?"

"Sure do. Dibs on the red car."

Steve said nothing.

Dodgem cars skated. The rides were long. Normally, there would have been lines and hungry eyes feeding on the riders.

"Hey, watch it, morons!" Helen didn't appreciate being sandwiched.

Too late. Her car bounced off the thick, rubber wall and spun out.

"Rotten jerks!"

They tried everything.

13

"Again!" whooped Jarvo as they got off the roller coaster.

"Nah, the tumbler!"

They forgot that there should have been attendants, that rides don't start and stop by themselves. They also forgot that old saying, the one about time and what happens to it when you're having fun.

"Now what?" Helen dragged them away from the wild west round-up.

"Girls' choice!" shouted Jodee.

The Ferris wheel scooped up the night in huge, silent hands.

"There!" pointed Spike. "Told you I saw the city!"

Ride after ride, hour after hour slipped by. They laughed at their reflections in the fun house. They rode helter-skelter down the slippery slide.

Suddenly, Steve shouted. He pointed to his wrist and shouted again. At ten to midnight there was only one ride left.

Slapstick ghouls and grinning skeletons adorned the ghost train building.

"This doesn't look scary." Jarvo ran up the stairs.

Larry studied the others. "It's okay before midnight, right?"

"Before midnight's fine," said Spike. "We all heard him."

"Right, so let's do it!"

Something whirred. Something clicked. A cartoon train rolled into view. Jarvo laughed. "Real scary, gang." He bit his lip in mock terror. "Hope we don't die . . . laughing."

The train stopped short of a painted black tunnel. Jarvo and Spike climbed aboard. More whirring and clicking; two identical trains appeared.

"Dibs on the second." Helen and Jodee climbed in.

"Guess that leaves only you and me." Larry pretend-punched the scaredy-cat. "Let's go, Steve."

As they stepped forward, three more empty trains arrived.

Wild laughter and fake screams looped in the dark. Wherever it was . . .

"Eeesh!"

Steve knew the bogeyman would get him.

"Weak!" shouted Larry.

Another kink in the track. A glow-in-the-dark monster mask jumped out from nowhere.

"So stuffed!"

Steve kicked himself and joined in the fun. Imagine being scared of this.

Back on the platform, Steve's watch beeped. Midnight.

Jarvo made a sudden announcement. "Again! Let's do it again!"

"You're kidding, right?" Steve looked at the others.

"Shut up, Steve." Larry stepped forward.

Past midnight. The six empty trains reappeared.

"Aw, what the heck!" Jarvo jumped into the first train. "Let's get this over with."

Steve grinned and climbed aboard. Again, Jodee and Helen grabbed the second train. Larry was already getting into the third.

Steve imagined the sharpest fangs. That painted black tunnel wanted to chop out the light forever.

And then their second ride was over.

"We made it!" shouted Steve. "We're still alive!"

"Dumbo! We got ripped off, that's all." Jarvo kicked the air. "The old guy was laughing at us."

"Hey, what gives?" asked Jodee.

Someone had shut the lights off.

"I want to go home," said Helen.

Steve looked at his watch. "Seven past midnight."

"Relax, Cinderella."

"Funny, ha-ha. But you've forgotten something. The last train home leaves at 12:15."

At the turnstile they found a brown envelope.

"The money!" Larry nearly choked.

They squeezed through the gates and started to run. Only . . .

Steve tripped and fell.

"Leave him!" shouted Jarvo.

The others stopped to pick him up.

They reached the station seconds too late. Two red lights disappeared along the track.

"Great," moaned Helen. "There goes our ride home."

Jarvo walked up to Steve and shoved him in the chest. "It's your fault, jerk!"

Larry and Spike pulled them apart. Further up the line they heard a whistle.

"Another train!" shouted Jodee.

Steve shook his watch. A splinter of light approached the station.

"Looks like you need a new watch battery," said Larry.

"Or a new face." Jarvo was still breathing hard.

The tracks pinged. The train slowed beside them.

"Hey, take a look at that," Jarvo hooted. "Well, well, well."

There, seated alone, sat the weirdo.

They boarded and Jarvo marched over. "Hey, pal, you're crazy."

The train pulled away. Larry and Spike joined Jarvo; Helen and Jodee found a seat and watched. Steve sat by himself.

"Hey, did you hear what I said?" Jarvo stood over the old man.

"Leave him alone." Larry didn't need this. "We got his money, right?"

"Station's coming up," warned Spike.

Jarvo wasn't listening. "Hey, old man, I'm talking to you. You were wrong. Nothing happened."

They pulled into the station. Everything looked strange, unreal.

"Fools," hissed the old man in a sinister voice. "I told you not to ride the ghost train after midnight."

Jarvo sneered. "Aw, that old ghost train didn't do anything."

"It wasn't that train I meant." The weirdo slowly lifted his face.

"All aboard!"

Every head snapped sideways.

Six pale figures stepped out of the darkness, clothes a ragged mess. Their whitewashed faces showed no emotion.

"It's those kids," said Steve. "Those six missing kids."

"My children," said the stranger. "They've been dying to meet you."

20

"No way!" Steve shut his eyes as the six ghostly visitors passed through the metal skin of the train.

A guard's whistle blew. Its note was long and endless, like the night.

The Mouth

The author
Allan Baillie
talks about the story

"It is lovely to be evil. In other stories I
have been very respectable with
flowers sprinkling around my computer,
but not with *The Mouth!* From the
moment I thought of it, I hunched over
the keyboard, drooling and cackling. I
would get the readers — all of them —
fool them, trap them, scare them. They
would never get away."

Allan Baillie

The Mouth

They were trailing home after school on a hot, breezeless afternoon. Anne-Marie, pounding the pavement flat; Steven, drooping, dragging his bag behind him; Neta, running her fingers along the fence as if it were a grand piano. And Luce, The Mouth.

Anne-Marie was talking about how unfair her mom was, blaming her for letting her brother wreck the eggbeater in the mud. But Steven and Neta were waiting for Luce to use The Mouth again.

"Just because I wasn't watching the ratty little kid," said Anne-Marie.

"They're all like that," Steven said. "They never listen to anything you say."

"My mom even makes me pick up the kid's toys, like they were mine," Neta said.

"They nag at you the minute you come in the door," said Steven bleakly.

Anne-Marie looked sideways at Luce. "And your mom?"

"What, me?"

"Your mom. What's she like?"

Luce opened her mouth, then sighed. "Oh, she's a witch."

The Mouth at work.

But Neta was disappointed. "That's all?"

"A terrible witch."

Luce was useful enough. She would help anyone anytime with anything, even math homework. But she had a very bad mouth, and it was almost on vacation today.

"Yeah, they get that way," said Anne-Marie.

A week ago, Luce had said, "Anne-Marie was the worst in the school play — forgot her lines, her dress sagged, she was nervous the whole time. The teachers didn't want to look."

Anne-Marie had pushed Luce into a deep puddle then, but that was a week ago.

"So you don't like your mom?" said Neta.

Luce had said Neta's party last month was "Boring. The record player hissed most of the time, and the cake was soggy. Steven was asleep in the corner . . ." Neta and Steven had sworn never to speak to Luce ever again. But that was a month ago.

"Oh no," said Luce.

"Only sometimes," said Steven. "I know, I know."

"But other times she's a witch," said Neta. "Yeah, sometimes I'd like to trade mine in."

"So when don't you like your mom, Luce?" said Steven. "When she makes you weed the garden?"

Luce stopped and stared blackly down the street. "When she makes me bring home the groceries for Dad."

"You're kidding! You don't know how easy you've got it."

"Special groceries. Every month. I shouldn't have to do it . . . " Luce thumped a post and strode off.

Anne-Marie played hopscotch on the pavement. "For your dad? Dads aren't much better. Mine ignores me and reads the paper."

"Mine throws things at me and roars," said Neta.

"Mine talks endlessly," said Anne-Marie.

"Mine's a monster," said Luce.

"That bad?" Anne-Marie said.

"Bad? Well, mainly at dinner," said Luce, stopping by her gate.

"Mine belches, even when there are visitors around." Steven shuddered.

"Don't you hate your family when they do something like that?" Neta said.

"Only my kid brother," Luce said and glared at the house. "All the time."

"Goes without saying," Anne-Marie said. "They all ought to be exterminated."

"Can't," Luce said sadly. "Want to come in?"

"Sure." Steven stepped into the yard. "What's your brother like?"

"He's a mean and nasty gnome." Luce led the way to the house.

They trooped into the house as Luce called for her mother. A voice called from a steamy kitchen in the back of the house. A plump woman was tasting a casserole in a glass dish, waving a wooden spoon.

"I brought some friends home," Luce said.

"That's nice." Luce's mom wiped her floury hands on her apron and introduced herself. "Would you like a snack?"

"Well . . ." Steven thought with his stomach.

"Of course you would! Tell you what, I'll fix something while Luce shows you the back yard. All right?"

Luce looked at her mother sourly.

"I think your father is down there."

"Oh, great." Luce stamped heavily out of the house.

Anne-Marie marched after Luce into a small orchard — orange, lemon, plum, apricot trees. "I think she's okay, your mom."

"When she's not mad at someone." Luce kicked through long grass.

Luce's mom called out from the house: "See if you can find a toad, dear."

Luce led Anne-Marie, Steven, and Neta through the lush orchard, light giving way to shade with long grass whispering in the breeze. She stopped

before a still pond with an ugly garden gnome glaring across the water.

"Hey," Steven said with a laugh. "There's Luce's brother!"

"Yes," Luce said without a smile. "I hope he grows moss."

The gnome's lips were curled back in a sneer that distorted an already mean face.

"It's a terrible gnome," said Anne-Marie.

"Worse when he gets to move around," said Luce.

Steven stared at the stone figure. "*Move* around?"

"In about a year." Neta laughed.

"How is he going to do that?"

"Oh, the spell wears off."

"The spell? *Spell?*"

"Mom put the spell on him when he went and put the spell on me. They can't be taken off. Both spells have to wear off."

The silence spread around the pond, leaving only the sounds of whispering grass and a quiet thumping.

Neta laughed again, but with a nervous edge.

"The gnome," Steven murmured. "I think it blinked at me."

There was no sound except for the whispering grass, the slow thumping, and something slithering.

"Don't be silly, Steven," said Anne-Marie. "She's making fun of us."

A bush quivered.

"Anyway, Luce, what spell is the gnome supposed to have put on you?" said Neta.

Thump.

"I was telling him fibs for fun. He got mad. So I now have to tell the whole truth. Every time."

Slither . . .

Steven blinked at Luce. So Luce said her mom was a witch and she *was* a witch. She said her brother was a gnome . . .

Steven's eyes grew wide. "What did you say about your dad?"

A heavy, wet sigh.

Luce stepped sideways and presented her friends. "Hi, Dad. Groceries."

The **Map Desk**

The author
Meredith Costain
talks about the story

"I was walking home one day when I saw one of those student desks with a map of the world on it outside a store. I started thinking about what would happen if you scribbled and scratched away at the countries. By the time I got home, I had the idea for the story."

Meredith Cost

The Map Desk

Adam Carter stomped into his room, steaming with anger. Rotten parents. Rotten school. Rotten, rotten homework.

The soccer finals were on TV. Everyone except Adam would be watching. He'd be sitting in his cold bedroom, with his books and his folders and his pencils, doing his homework. It just wasn't fair.

Adam stared at the surface of his desk. Anything to take his mind off math. The desk was old, a present from his weirdo uncle, Aldo. Aldo never came to visit much, but when he did, he always brought a gift for someone in the family. Then he'd disappear again, off on his travels. The desk had sturdy legs, and three small drawers down one side. "For your secret treasures," Uncle Aldo had winked. "Use it wisely, now." But Adam had filled the drawers with stubby, old pencils, with broken leads, crumpled pieces of paper, and lumps of stale chewing gum. Adam didn't believe in secrets *or* treasures.

The most special thing about Uncle Aldo's desk was the top, with its large, colorful map of the world. Africa beckoned, a dark and mysterious red. Cool, blue seas washed the shores of the shell-pink islands of the Pacific. The purple boot of Italy kicked poor Sicily into the Mediterranean. Wish *I* was in Italy, thought Adam, as he struggled with his sums. Bet *their* parents don't make them do homework when the soccer finals are on. He doodled with the point of his compass on the long tip of the tiny country. Little flakes of purple paint piled up on the desktop. It was no good. He just

didn't *feel* like doing sums. Not while the soccer game was on.

"Look at this," said his father at breakfast the next morning. He waggled the newspaper. "There was a massive landslide in southern Italy yesterday. Hundreds of homes were buried. Isn't this the village your grandmother came from, Anna?"

"Not that one, no," said Adam's mother, peering at the front page news story. "Nonna lived near Brindisi. But, it must have been terrible for all of those people. Terrible." She turned to Adam, who was eating his cereal hungrily. "Did you finish your homework, Adam?"

"We-ell . . . " began Adam.

"Then you'll have to do double tonight," said his mother. "Understand?"

Boy, was she a slave driver!

There was a live broadcast of the football game on TV that night. Adam decided to do his homework right after school, rather than after dinner. That way he might be finished in time for his program. He sped through his science assignment, raced through his reading review, and was just reaching for his geography book when his elbow made contact with the glass of juice balancing on the corner of his desk.

"Shoot!" said Adam. The juice soaked into his science project, smudging the tricky diagram he'd just spent hours perfecting. A little puddle of juice flowed over onto the surface of the desk, but he was too concerned with saving his precious drawing to notice.

"Mooommm!" he wailed. He carried the soaked paper into the kitchen. Mrs. Carter studied the ruined project. "It's no use carrying on about it, Adam," she said. "You'll just have to do it again. Come on. It's not the end of the world."

"Well, it is for me," muttered Adam. The project was due the next day. He'd have to do the diagram all over again and miss the football game. Rotten homework.

"Call your sister for dinner, Adam." Adam flounced into the living room. The news was on. "... *and in California, people are fleeing coastal towns in droves as tidal waves threaten the southwest coast.*" Adam watched the flickering images on the screen. His brow wrinkled for a moment. Tidal waves? There was always some disaster happening in the world. "Dinner!" he called, plonking himself down at the table.

Half an hour later he was back at his desk again. He took out a fresh piece of paper and unzipped his pencil case. The little puddle of juice stared accusingly at him from the map of North America. He soaked it up with the sleeve of his sweater and started in again on his diagram. But the drawing wouldn't come out right.

"Rotten homework," muttered Adam. He used his black marker to slowly and painstakingly obliterate a tiny principality in Central Europe. Bet they don't have to do homework in that American flooded place, he thought, widening the circle of black marks carefully. He drew a ring of little dots around the black blot. Then he put away his books and went to bed.

The next morning, the papers were full of a tragedy in Europe. A massive earthquake had struck overnight, annihilating the population of an entire country. "Such terrible things that happen in the world," said Adam's mother, shaking her head.

"Where was it *this* time?" asked Adam, his mouth full of cornflakes.

"A tiny little country in Europe," said his mother. "And now there's nothing. Just a black hole in the map."

A hole? A *black* hole? Adam wiped his mouth with his sleeve and pulled the newspaper toward him. He studied the map on the front page showing where the country had been. After a moment he excused himself from the table and, knees trembling, headed for his bedroom.

He looked down at the map desk. He compared the position of the black marks he had made the night before with the map in the newspaper. A tiny alarm bell pinged in his brain. He looked down again at the map. The surface over California was still slightly sticky from the hastily mopped up juice. The purple toe of Italy was flaking and peeling. It was just as if . . .

No. It couldn't be. He *couldn't* be controlling the events of the world. Could he? Adam looked down at the map. The brightly colored countries looked back trustingly at him. No. It wasn't possible.

But he longed to experiment, to test out his theory. Just one little, insignificant country. One that no one had ever heard of. The power. Just think of the power! He wouldn't ever have to do homework again!

Adam pored over the map, looking for a place that no one would miss. Of course! Antarctica! Antarctica was just one gigantic block of ice, wasn't it? Surely no one would miss a few acres of ice.

He reached into the bottom desk drawer and pulled out a box of matches. Slowly, carefully, he lit one and held the blue flame to the white mass at the bottom of the map. The paint hissed and fizzed, and the match glowed brightly before blackening and dying. No homework tonight! thought Adam gleefully.

Adam was the first to breakfast. He grabbed the paper from the front step, ripping it open with trembling hands. "Polar ice caps melting!" blazed the headline. "Threat to low-level countries."

It was true! It worked! He could control the world. All through school his mind rattled and hummed, plotting and planning his future. He would be powerful. Powerful and rich. Kings and presidents would vie for his powers. He couldn't wait for school to end, so he could get back to his precious map desk and play with the world.

As Adam hurried through his front door, he heard a curious buzzing sound. *Bzzzz.* Pause. *Bzzzz.* The rasping sound filled the house with noise. "Is that you, Adam?" his mother called. "Come here, young man, I want to talk to you."

Adam was in a hurry to get to his room, to his map desk, to his world. "Later, Mom, all right? I've got some homework to do."

"Well, that's what I want to talk to you about," said his mother, coming up close to him. "That lovely desk your Uncle Aldo gave you. You've been ruining it, just like a little vandal. It's all scratched and scribbled on."

Adam paused, one hand on the door of his bedroom. The rasping sound was growing louder.

"It's a mess. And it must be distracting you from your homework. So I've asked your father to clean it up for you."

The rasping sound was now unbearably loud. The whine of an electric motor drowned out the scream that launched itself from Adam's throat.

"Nnnooooooo . . . !" he shrieked, throwing open the door. The buzzing sound stopped abruptly, as Mr. Carter switched off his electric sander and turned to face his son. But it was too late. Already, the edges of the room were slowly beginning to darken . . .

About the Illustrators

The Story Illustrator
Richard Morden

Richard Morden is a commercial artist. As he lives with his wife, her son, a badly adjusted rat, and a dwarf rabbit, he feels highly qualified to illustrate these spooky tales. Richard wants nothing more in life than to illustrate and to keep from being turned into a newt!

The Cover Illustrator
Marc McBride

Marc McBride has illustrated covers for several magazines and children's books. Marc currently creates the realistic images for his covers using acrylic ink with an airbrush. To solve his messy studio problem, he plans to use computer graphics instead.